Girls Play to Win

SKIING &
SNOWBOARDING

by Karen L. Kenney

Content Consultant
Frida Waara

U.S. National Ski
& Snowboard
Hall of Fame
Board of Directors

NORWOOD HOUSE PRESS
CHICAGO, ILLINOIS

Norwood House Press
P.O. Box 316598
Chicago, Illinois 60631

For information regarding Norwood House Press, please visit our website at:
www.norwoodhousepress.com or call 866-565-2900.

Photo Credits: Ben Blankenburg/iStockphoto, cover, 1, 8; Marco Trovati/AP Images, 4;
iStockphoto, 5, 15; Val Thoermer/Fotolia, 7; Steve Debenport/iStockphoto, 11; Fotolia,
12, 38; William Henry Jackson/Library of Congress, 16; Library of Congress, 18; AP
Images, 21, 22, 24; Tony Talbot/AP Images, 27; Gerry Broome/AP Images, 28; Close
Encounters Photography/Shutterstock Images, 30; Andrey Artykov/iStockphoto, 32;
Paco Ayala/Fotolia, 35; Alena Kovalenko/Fotolia, 36; Robert F. Bukaty/AP Images,
41, 43; Rudi Blaha/AP Images, 44; Douglas C. Pizac/AP Images, 49; Gero Breloer/AP
Images, 50; Frank Gunn/AP Images, 52; Nathan Bilow/AP Images, 53; Mario Sanchez/
AP Images, 57; Karen Kenney, 64 (top); Frida Waara, 64 (bottom)

Editor: Melissa Johnson
Designer: Christa Schneider
Project Management: Red Line Editorial

Library of Congress Cataloging-in-Publication Data

Kenney, Karen Latchana.
  Girls play to win skiing and snowboarding / By Karen Latchana Kenney.
    p. cm. — (Girls play to win)
  Includes bibliographical references and index.
  Summary: "Covers the history, rules, fundamentals and significant
personalities of the sports of women's skiing and snowboarding. Topics
include: techniques, strategies, competitive events, and equipment.
Glossary, Additional Resources and Index included"—Provided by publisher.
  ISBN-13: 978-1-59953-391-9 (library edition : alk. paper)
  ISBN-10: 1-59953-391-X (library edition : alk. paper)
  1. Women skiers—Juvenile literature. 2. Snowboarding—Juvenile
literature. I. Title.
  GV854.34.K46 2010
  796.93082—dc22

                    2010009808

Manufactured in the United States of America in North Mankato, Minnesota.
157N—072010

Girls Play to Win
SKIING &
SNOWBOARDING

Table of Contents

▲ Lindsey Vonn skis to a third-place finish in a World Cup **super-combined** event in 2010.

CHAPTER 1

SKIING
BASICS

Olympic gold medalist Lindsey Vonn wears a lot of pink. But don't think she's not tough. Vonn is confident and fearless, hurtling herself down mountainsides at more than 65 miles per hour (105 kph)—faster than a car on a highway. Few **elite** skiers can compete and win in every **alpine** event like Vonn does.

Vonn is also well known for **perseverance**. She has dedicated her life to training to reach her peak performance.

Careful and determined training also has allowed her to recover fully from several skiing injuries. Vonn won the U.S. Olympic Committee's Olympic Spirit Award at the 2006 Olympics. She crashed during a practice run but recovered in time to compete in the **downhill** event and finish in the top ten. Vonn's motto is, "If you work hard, it will pay off in the end."

Vonn serves as an example and inspiration for athletes everywhere. Above all, Vonn shows how much fun it is to ski. From the beginner picking up poles for the first time to the teenaged girl who's poised to be the next Lindsey Vonn, everyone can enjoy the ride.

GETTING STARTED

Skiing sports include downhill, cross-country, and

Skiers make tight turns around gates that mark their courses.

SKIING LINGO:

alpine: *Downhill skiing.*

fall line: *The fastest way to go down the hill.*

gate: *The markers that indicate the race course.*

moguls: *Bumps on the ski slope.*

Nordic: *Cross-country skiing.*

powder: *Light, fluffy new snow.*

slalom: *To ski or zigzag between gates. Slalom is also a specific alpine skiing event; it has the most gates of all the alpine events.*

Learning to Ski

The best way to learn how to ski is to take a lesson. With a good teacher, you can learn to ski in as little as an afternoon. Here are some things you can expect to learn in your first lesson:

1. First, your instructor will probably have you get a feel for your skis. Moving with long, flat things attached to your feet takes a little getting used to.

2. Next, you may practice gliding forward. Gliding is the basic action you need if you want to go anywhere.

3. Next, you'll probably learn how to stop. Knowing how to stop the right way can help you avoid injuries.

4. Your instructor will also help you practice getting back up. Everybody falls—even professionals. Laugh about it, brush the snow off, and keep going!

freestyle. Most people learn to ski downhill or cross-country first. Freestyle, which is full of jumps and tricks, is for more advanced skiers.

DOWNHILL

Downhill skiing, or alpine skiing, is done on big hills or mountains. Many skiers go to ski areas or resorts to downhill ski. The slopes are groomed to work well for skiing sports. They can be covered with powder or hard-packed snow.

▲ *Cross-country skiers use poles to help move themselves forward. This woman is skiing skate style.*

FREESTYLE

In freestyle, the skier moves over **moguls** (small hills on a course) or performs flips, twists, and spins off a jump. Different freestyle moves include the backscratcher, back-flip, alley oop, and many more.

CROSS-COUNTRY

In cross-country skiing, also called **Nordic** skiing, skiers travel over groomed trails or make their own tracks out in the country. Cross-country skiing takes a lot of effort because skiers move mostly under their own power.

There are two styles of cross-country skiing. In the classical style, also called diagonal style, skiers kick and glide their skis forward along two grooves in the snow. The skier needs long skis and poles that come up to her underarms for this style.

▲ Some freestyle skiers perform jumps and tricks in the air.

In freestyle cross-country skiing, also called skate skiing, the skiers move as if they are ice-skating. Freestyle skiing needs flat, hard snow. The skis are shorter than classical skis, and the poles are longer, running from the skier's chin to the ground.

THE RIGHT DOWNHILL SKIS

A downhill skier needs to think about several different factors when choosing her skis. Does she like to ski very fast down the hill or make quick turns? Does she like to do tricks or ski on powder? A new skier might begin with learner skis that are easier to control. Some companies make skis that are designed specifically for women. Once a skier knows her favorite skiing style, she can choose the right skis.

Downhill skis have some basic elements. These parts of the ski are changed slightly to make them perfect for specific kinds of skiing.

- A downhill ski has an hourglass shape. The tip and tail are wider than the middle, called the waist. The shape and size of the waist affects how the ski turns.

- The ski's metal edges help **carve** the turn when the ski is at an angle.

- The bottom of the ski needs to glide smoothly on the snow. It is covered in polyethylene, which is a type of plastic that is tough and light.

Alpine vs. Nordic Gear

The first major difference between alpine and Nordic skiing is the skis. In alpine skiing, boots are attached to the skis at the heels and toes. In Nordic skiing, however, only the toe is attached. Nordic skis are generally lighter and narrower than alpine skis. Nordic skis need different wax than alpine skis, too.

Alpine ski boots are made of hard plastic. They are heavy and rigid. Nordic ski boots are lighter and more flexible. In general, Nordic gear is designed to be lighter than alpine gear. Nordic skiers have to propel themselves, so skiers do everything possible to make the load lighter. Alpine skiers can wear heavy, waterproof pants and jackets. Nordic skiers need to carefully choose layers that will keep them warm and dry without making them too hot and sweaty.

- The **camber** of the ski is the way it is curved up in the middle on its profile. Putting pressure on this part of the ski also affects how a skier turns on the snow.

DOWNHILL SKIERS ALSO NEED A FEW OTHER PIECES OF EQUIPMENT:

- Bindings fit on top of the skis. The bindings of downhill skis have toe and heel pieces. The bindings lock the skier's boots onto the skis. If the skier falls, the bindings release the boots to reduce the chance of injury.

▲ *Downhill skis, boots, and bindings*

- Special boots fit into the bindings. They support the skier's feet and help steer the skis.

- Poles are long, light, and strong. They help the skier steer or move more quickly.

- Skis must be waxed to perform well. The temperature and moisture of the snow determines which wax the skier should use.

- Skiers also need proper outerwear to protect them from the wind and cold and a helmet to protect them from head injuries. All skiers should also wear sunglasses or goggles to protect their eyes. Lip balm and sunscreen protect skiers' skin.

▲ *This skier has all the gear she needs—poles (1) and skis (2), boots (3) and bindings (4), warm clothing (5), goggles (6), and a helmet (7).*

COMPETITIONS

Once you have mastered the basics of skiing, you might want to try competing. Young skiers can join ski clubs or school ski teams. Nordic, alpine, and freestyle skiing competitions each have multiple events.

The alpine ski events are **slalom**, **giant slalom**, **super-G**, and downhill. In each, the skier must maneuver around **gates** as quickly as possible. The difference between the events is the number and placement of gates. Slalom has the most gates, which means the skier must be able to make the tightest and most difficult turns. Giant slalom has fewer gates than slalom. Super-G has the next fewest gates. Downhill has the fewest gates of all. Downhill skiers must still navigate around gates. But with fewer turns, the focus of the event is speed. Advanced downhill skiers easily hit speeds above 60 miles per hour (97 kph). The super-combined event includes one downhill and one slalom race.

Freestyle skiing events include moguls, aerials, ski cross, and ski jumping. In mogul events, skiers are judged on speed and style as they ski between moguls while staying in the **fall line**. In aerial events, skiers fly off jumps. While in the air, they perform flips and twists before landing. In ski cross, four skiers race at the same time over a course that includes jumps and turns. In ski jumping, skiers slide down a high ramp and glide as far as possible through the air. Skiers are judged on distance and style. Even through the first decade of the 21st century, ski jumping was not an Olympic event for women. It was part of the World Championships, however.

Cross-country skiers compete using the classical (diagonal) technique or the freestyle (skate) technique. Races can also be a combination of the two. Distances are measured in kilometers, and can be anywhere from 5K to 50K (3.1 to 31 miles). Some races are sprints, in which a skier shows how fast she can ski a short distance. Other races involve one or many people racing on a long-distance course. In still other races, skiers compete in pairs or in relays of four. Skiers in Nordic combined events must ski a cross-country race and complete a ski jump.

Professional Competitions

There are three major competitions for professional female skiers:

International Ski Federation (FIS) World Cup: This competition lasts through an entire skiing season. Athletes compete in several races and are judged by how well they perform over the entire season. The World Cup is held every year.

FIS World Championships: This competition takes place every other year over a two-week period, usually in February.

Olympic Winter Games: This competition is held every four years, usually in February. The Olympic Winter Games feature many winter sports, including skiing and snowboarding.

▲ *A skier makes a tight turn around a gate in an alpine event.*

▲ *Members of the Goldi tribe in Russia hunted on skis like these.*

CHAPTER 2

THE NEED TO SKI

The first skis appeared thousands of years ago, invented by prehistoric people in cold, snowy regions. To these people, skiing was not a sport; it was a necessity. Using skis allowed them to cross frozen wetlands and travel greater distances. People living in mountain areas needed skis to go anywhere quickly in winter. Hunters on skis chased elk to feed their families in the long winter months. Cave paintings show these early skiers in hunting scenes. In those times, skiing was an important skill for survival.

Prehistoric people even developed different styles of skis to perform best in local conditions. Ancient skis from areas with more powdery snow were different than skis from areas prone to hard-packed snow or ice.

FROM NECESSITY TO SPORT

Skiing has been a part of Scandinavian culture for thousands of years. Scandinavia includes the countries of Norway, Finland, and Sweden. Norwegian soldiers were trained in cross-country skiing. These ski troops were holding organized ski races by the 1700s, if not earlier. Ski racing started becoming popular with ordinary citizens in the 1800s. Norwegians took pride in their skiing traditions, and ski clubs soon appeared around the country.

Birkebeiner Race

Skis have been used in war since the 13th century or earlier. In 1206, a civil war raged in Norway. Two members of a group of soldiers called the Birkebeiners (for their birch-bark shin guards) rescued Norway's infant prince and skied him 33 miles (54 km) to safety. The daring feat inspired several modern long-distance cross-country races. They are named Birkebeiner in remembrance.

In the 19th century and earlier, women wore corsets like this one under their dresses.

CHANGING SKI CLOTHING

*The clothing worn by female skiers in the late 1800s put them at a disadvantage. At the time, it was considered proper for women to wear a **corset**, long skirt, and long coat while skiing. Wearing corsets restricted women's lungs, making it hard for them to breathe. This was the first piece of clothing the women stopped wearing while skiing. Then, in 1892, Eva Nansen dared to wear pants under a shorter skirt while skiing. It made skiing much easier. By the 1920s, most women wore pants, not skirts, while skiing.*

The first recorded ski race that included a woman was held by the Trysil Rifle and Skiing Club on January 21, 1863. The woman was 16 years old, and her name was Ingrid Olsdatter Vestbyen. Ingrid raced well—better than some of the men—and was cheered on by the watching crowd. She was not an official competitor in the race, but people noticed her skill and ability. Trysil and other early ski clubs only allowed men. Women's ski clubs were first formed in the late 1800s.

On March 1, 1891, the Asker Ski Club held its annual ski race, and women were asked to participate for the first time. Female skiers competed in a separate race from the men. The winner was Hannah Aars, who won a gold pin as her prize. This race is considered the first event in modern women's ski racing.

SERIOUS COMPETITION

Skiing soon spread to other countries, and new athletes emerged in the sport. In 1908, an international ski race that included women was held in Chamonix, France. It was the first of its kind. Women also began competing in ski clubs and on college teams.

In 1931, the first annual World Championships was held. It included ski events for men and for women. Alpine racing became an event for women and men in the Olympic Winter Games in 1936. The 1936 Olympics only had one women's ski event, a combined event with one downhill and two slalom races. The clear champion was German athlete Cristl Cranz. She also won every World Championship title between 1934 and 1939.

The United States sent a female ski team to the first Olympic skiing competition in 1936. Team member Betty Woolsey took 14th place. Gretchen Fraser would win the first U.S. gold medal in skiing in 1948.

Cross-Country Competitions

At the beginning of the 20th century, cross-country skiing was seen as a man's sport. The races were long, and the athletes needed high endurance to compete. At that time in history, many people believed that women could not compete in athletic events that needed great strength and endurance. It took many years for women to be accepted in cross-country skiing competitions. Early women's competitions were held in the 1920s and 1930s in Norway and Finland. In 1952, cross-country skiing was added as a women's event in the Olympic Winter Games. The first winner of the gold medal was Lydia Widman, a woman from Finland.

The giant slalom was added as an Olympic ski event in 1952. That year, Andrea Mead Lawrence became the first American to win two gold medals at the Olympics. She won the slalom and the giant slalom events. With these wins, the United States became a serious contender in competitive skiing.

▲ In 1948, Gretchen Fraser became the first U.S. woman to win an Olympic gold medal in skiing, winning the women's slalom event.

▲ *Canadian Nancy Greene
won the first World Cup in 1967.*

CHAPTER 3

SKIING EVOLVES

Since 1912, skis have continued to get lighter and stronger as technology has improved. Metal strips were added to skis' edges. This helped skiers go down steep mountains on hard snow. In the early 1950s, metal skis were created. They allowed skiers to turn easily without twisting their skis. Then, **fiberglass** skis came out in the mid-1950s. These skis were lighter and even easier to turn than the metal ones.

Other ski equipment changed as well. Bamboo and steel poles were replaced with lighter, stronger aluminum poles. New boots were made from hard, molded plastic. These stronger boots gave skiers more support and allowed them to turn more easily. All this new equipment helped skiers ski faster and with more control, and athletes improved in the sport.

Getting Up the Hill

In the early days of the sport, a quick run down the mountain meant a long hike back to the top. The invention of the rope tow made getting back up the hill a lot easier. Motors moved a rope up the hill. Skiers grabbed on to the rope and were pulled to the top. The rope was hard to hang on to, though. Most historians agree that the first rope tow appeared in Germany in 1908. However, it didn't catch on in other places. The first rope tows in North America were invented independently from the European version in the 1930s.

The chairlift, still used today, was invented in 1936. It replaced most rope tows in resorts worldwide by the 1950s. Artificial snow was invented in 1954, allowing resorts to keep the slopes open even when the weather did not cooperate. Other new machines smoothed out the snow. Many ski resorts were built in the 1950s and 1960s, giving skiers more places to go. More women also started skiing in the 1960s and 1970s. The sport has become increasingly popular every year.

▲ *An early-1960s model displays stretch ski pants.*

A new clothing style for women was seen on the slopes in 1952. New technology allowed clothing factories to create threads that mixed wool with artificial fibers such as nylon. This new type of thread created a stretchy fabric. Maria Bogner, a German woman, used this new fabric to make ski pants that stretched. Skiing women loved the new stretch pants. Famous actresses such as Marilyn Monroe and Ingrid Bergman were seen in Bogner's skiing fashion.

MORE SKIERS, BETTER COMPETITIONS

The competitive skiing season lasts the entire winter. Sometimes, skiers perform well at one race but do poorly at the next. In 1967, the World Cup was created to judge alpine skiers' performance through the whole season. Skiers would compete in a series of races in several countries, and the person with the most points would be the champion. The first female World Cup winner was Nancy Greene of Canada. She won this competition a second time in 1968. The World Cup has since grown to include other types of skiing and snowboarding.

For cross-country skiing, the 1970s marked the beginning of change. People became more concerned with their health. They saw the sport as a way to stay fit and healthy. Cross-country skiing became very popular. Long ski races called **marathons** had been run in Norway for decades. Now, new ski marathons emerged around the world. The Wisconsin Birkebeiner, a 54-kilometer (33 mile) cross-country ski race, started in 1973. Soon, 9,000 competitors were participating in this annual race. Although cross-country skiing has become popular in North America, Europeans still win most of the competitions.

A NEW STYLE

The 1960s was a time of change in the United States. Americans were trying many new things. In alpine skiing, they performed new tricks and stunts to create a new style—freestyle. At first, it was called "hotdogging," because the sport was an edgy, showoff type of skiing.

Men's freestyle competitions started in the mid-1960s. In 1971, Suzy Chaffee was the first woman to compete. The World Cup added freestyle in 1980, with events for men and women. U.S. skier Jan Bucher was the champion. She won this competition seven times in the 1980s.

Moguls were added as an event in the Olympic Winter Games in 1992, and aerials were added two years later. Donna Weinbrecht of the United States was the first female gold medalist in the moguls. The first woman to win the gold in the aerials was Lina Tcherjazova of Uzbekistan.

From Skates to Skis

U.S. freestyle skier Jan Bucher started as a competitive figure skater, but an ankle injury at age 17 prevented her from reaching the top in that sport. At age 20, she met some freestyle skiers who suggested she try skiing. Bucher found that many skating tricks translated well to skis: "Things the skiers had been working on for years, I could do really quick, because it was the same kind of stuff I'd been doing for almost all my life on skates. The big difference was now I had these long edges, where before I had teeny ones. It was much more stable." Bucher's skating influence took freestyle skiing to a new level in the 1980s.

▲ Freestyle skier Suzy Chaffee became a member of the U.S. National Ski Hall of Fame in 1988.

▲ Lindsey Jacobellis races in a
qualifying event at the 2010 Olympics.

CHAPTER 4

SNOWBOARDING BASICS

You don't have to ski to enjoy the snow. And you don't have to take first place to be a winner. Snowboarder Lindsey Jacobellis is considered one of the best **snowboard cross** riders in the world. She has multiple World Cup and World Championships victories. But, as of 2010, she had never won an Olympic gold medal.

Jacobellis was seconds from victory during the snowboard cross race in 2006 at the Olympics in Turin, Italy. In celebration, she attempted a showy move just before the finish line. She messed up, fell, and took home silver instead of gold.

After the Olympics, Jacobellis dusted off her snowpants and got back up on her board, winning multiple competitions in the four years between Olympic games. Going into the 2010 Olympics, she was heavily favored to take gold. **Media** commentators argued that she had to win to redeem herself from her fall in 2006.

During the race, however, Jacobellis went out of bounds and was disqualified. She finished in fifth place and with no Olympic medal. Jacobellis wouldn't let disappointment keep her down for long, though. "It's definitely not the end of the world for me," she said. "It's unfortunate that the rest of the world only sees this race and the one four years ago."

Jacobellis has great advice for beginning snowboarders, too. "If you fall, or make a mistake, you never stop trying until you cross the finish line because anything can happen."

GETTING STARTED

In some ways, snowboarding combines skateboarding with surfing on the snow. You can glide slowly down

This snowboarder grabs her board while getting air.

SNOWBOARDING LINGO

getting air: *Doing jumps on your snowboard.*

goofy-foot: *A rider who rides with his or her right foot forward.*

grab: *To grab your board while airborne.*

half-pipe: *A deep, rounded ramp with steep walls.*

hip: *A terrain-park feature; a steep ramp leading to a narrow plateau with another steep ramp on the other side, similar to a letter A with a flat top and sides rounded inward.*

rail: *A narrow, man-made feature made of wood or metal used for sliding.*

quarter-pipe: *A steep ramp; half of a half-pipe.*

slide: *To ride on the edge of something that is not snow. Another word for slide is grind.*

switch: *Riding backward.*

terrain park: *An area built for snowboarders to practice tricks.*

the slope or race quickly. Freestyle snowboarders do tricks and twists. Snowboarding can be done at most ski resorts or special snowboarding parks called **terrain parks**.

THE RIGHT SNOWBOARD

To get started snowboarding, you need to have the right gear. There are different types of boards, boots, and bindings.

Frontside or Backside?

Many snowboard tricks take their name from skateboarding or surfing. Many tricks that include **rotation** include the number of rotations in the name. Rotations are indicated in degrees. With 360 degrees in a full circle, a snowboarder goes 90 degrees every time she completes a quarter of a rotation. A 720 is two complete rotations, 900 is two-and-a-half rotations, and so on.

The names of many tricks also describe the direction of the rotation. Frontside means the snowboarder rotated facing forward. Backside means the snowboarder rotated with her back going first. The actual direction of the spin—clockwise or counterclockwise—depends if the snowboarder rides with her left or right foot first. In a **half-pipe**, frontside and backside can also refer to whether the rider is facing the wall (frontside) or has her back to the wall (backside).

▲ *This snowboarder is putting her boot in her snowboard's bindings. She has the rest of her gear too: helmet, warm clothes, and goggles.*

Snowboards have several basic elements:

- The two tips are called the nose (front) and the tail (back). They both tilt upward to help the board float on top of the snow.

- The middle part of the board, called the waist, is thinner than the tips. A board with a skinnier waist can make sharper turns.

- Sharp metal edges surround the board, helping it grip the snow during turns.

Snowboarders also need bindings and boots. Bindings connect the boots to the snowboard and help in steering, similar to skis. The spoiler is the high back part of the binding. It supports the boots and ankles and helps control the pressure on the board.

Boots can be soft or hard. Soft boots are easier to wear, which makes them good for new snowboarders. More advanced snowboarders can wear hard boots, which help them make precise movements on the snow.

Snowboarders, like skiers, must also choose outerwear to protect them from the snow and cold, including jacket, pants, hat, gloves, and goggles. Snowboarders

Dressed for Success

Whether you're speeding down the mountain or practicing tricks at the terrain park, you have to dress for outside winter weather. The best way to be prepared is to dress in layers. Wearing a cotton sweatshirt is a sure way to spend the afternoon shivering, as the cotton absorbs sweat and melted snow to make you cold and wet. Instead, begin with an under layer of **wicking fabric** to pull sweat and liquid away from your skin. Middle layers should be wool, fleece, or man-made materials to trap air and keep you **insulated** even if you get wet. Outer layers should protect you from wind and water without being too heavy or getting in the way of movement. Remember good socks, gloves, and, if it's really cold, a face mask.

also wear a helmet to protect them from head injuries. Sunscreen and lip balm protect their skin.

COMPETITIONS

Young snowboarders can join snowboarding clubs or school snowboarding teams to start snowboarding competitively. Snowboarding competitions involve different events.

The half-pipe event takes place in a large trench with two near-vertical side walls. Speed from riding the walls gets the snowboarder air for doing tricks.

Professional Competitions

There are many major competitions for professional female snowboarders. The Olympic Winter Games and the FIS World Cup and World Championships feature snowboarding events in addition to their skiing events. Other competitions include:

U.S. Open Snowboarding Championships: This event is held every year. In recent years, it has taken place in March. It is the oldest continuing snowboarding event in the world.

The Winter X Games: This competition is sponsored by ESPN and is held every year, usually in January. The X is short for "extreme." It also includes freestyle skiing events such as aerials and moguls.

▲ *A snowboarder turns around a gate.*

In slalom events, snowboarders race down the slope, turning around gates. In the parallel slalom, two courses run side by side. Two racers go down the courses at the same time.

The snowboard cross event has turns, jumps, and other challenges in the course. The first snowboarder to cross the finish line wins the race.

The big air event involves a big jump. While in the air, the athlete twists, rolls, spins, and grabs her board.

In **slopestyle** events, the snowboarder performs different tricks while racing down a course filled with jumps, **rails**, **hips**, and a half-pipe or **quarter-pipe**.

▲ *This snowboarder can hit the slopes because earlier women fought for acceptance in the sport.*

CHAPTER 5

SNOWBOARDING
HITS THE SCENE

Surfers ride waves on their boards. Skateboarders ride pavement. And snowboarders surf mountains. Skiers got the idea of snowboarding from surfers and learned the tricks of skateboarders. Snowboarding was a new and radical way to get down a mountain. It was also really fun. This new sport caught on quickly with a new generation of athletes.

EARLY SNOWBOARDING

Just as some prehistoric people used primitive skis to get around in the snow, some populations used a single board that is a distant relative of the modern snowboard. Throughout history, there are stories of individuals using boards in a similar fashion. However, these isolated examples did not catch on widely until very recently.

In 1965, Sherman Poppen wanted to make something for his two daughters to play with in the snow. He screwed two skis together to make one piece and tied a string to the tips. He called it the Snurfer, a combination of the words *snow* and *surfer*. It was later made as a plastic toy. Over the next ten years, he sold almost a million.

Dimitrije Milovich made the next version of the snowboard, the Winterstick, in his Utah garage in 1974. Tom Sims, a skateboarder, made his first snowboard in seventh-grade woodshop. He would later perform his skateboarding tricks in the snow. He started selling his boards in 1978. At the same time, Jake Burton was experimenting with snowboards. He had ridden the Snurfer as a kid. Burton was a snowboarder, and he was also a good businessman. The Snurfer, the Winterstick, and Burton's boards all contributed to the birth of the modern snowboard.

Early snowboarders were not received well by the skiing community. Many resorts banned snowboarders.

A snowboarder practices in a half-pipe.

THE HISTORY OF THE HALF-PIPE

In 1978, a group of high school kids spent their time riding their Winter-sticks in Tahoe City, California. They found a gully behind a garbage dump. When it snowed, the kids raced to the gully after school. They shoveled the snow to make the gully deep enough to ride. Then, they did their moves on the snow—moves that had only been done on skateboards before. This gully was the first recorded snowboarding half-pipe.

In 1982, pioneering snowboarder Tom Sims heard about the half-pipe and went to watch the high school kids perform their tricks. Sims was impressed. The kids were doing tricks he had seen in skateboarding, plus some that were totally new. He signed one of the kids to his pro team. Then, in 1983, Sims had a half-pipe made for the World Snowboarding Championships held in Soda Springs, California. It was the first snowboarding half-pipe competition.

Snowboarders were often perceived as young and disruptive, similar to the popular media portrayal of surfers and skateboarders. Women who wanted to snowboard had to work twice as hard. Not only did they have to find places where their boards were welcome, they also had to fight their way into a sport that was initially dominated by men.

GETTING COMPETITIVE

A small group of snowboarders including Burton held the first major U.S. snowboarding championship event in the winter of 1982—at the time, the event was known as the National Snow Surfing Championships. In later years, this contest would become known as the U.S. Open Snowboarding Championships. The first event was held in Vermont, and riders came from five other states. Women competed for the first time in 1984.

In 1983, Tom Sims held the World Snowboarding Championships in California. The two contests were very

Pro Teams

For snowboard makers, having their own pro teams is a great way to market their boards. When the teams' top athletes compete, it helps get out the word about the snowboard companies. Pro teams also help advance the sport. Athletes who are paid just to snowboard can concentrate on their sport. They become even better on the slopes.

The European Women

As snowboarding spread internationally, women were quick to pick it up. A West German, Petra Mussig, won the first World Cup. Europeans also took five out of six possible medals in the women's snowboarding events in the 1998 Olympic Winter Games. Karine Ruby of France won the giant slalom event. Through 12 years of competition in the World Cup, Ruby won an impressive 67 events. The winner of the 1998 Olympic half-pipe was German Nicola Thost. She was also the first woman to do back-to-back 720s (two 720 rotations in a row) in competition.

different. Burton's event was more like a race. Sims's involved skateboarding tricks, and he had a half-pipe built for the competition. These early contests helped snowboarding become the sport it is today—one of freestyle tricks and racing speed. The FIS has held the Snowboarding World Championships since 1997.

Snowboarding quickly caught on internationally. Japan also held its first national snowboarding contest in 1982. The European Championships were held four years later. The first Snowboarding World Cup was held during the winter of 1987–88, with both European and U.S. competitors. By the 1990s, most resorts welcomed snowboarders, and many had built terrain parks and other special features to attract them. Then, in 1998,

▲ German snowboarder Nicola Thost won the first Olympic gold medal for half-pipe in 1998.

snowboarding joined the Olympic Winter Games with two events—the half-pipe and the giant slalom.

WOMEN WIN AND GO PRO

At first, the best snowboarding athletes were mostly men, but a few women were also at the top of the game. In the late 1980s and early 1990s, the companies that made snowboards started putting together professional teams. These pro teams included the top snowboarding athletes at the time.

In 1988, Kemper Snowboards signed Tina Basich of the United States. She was the only female snowboarder on Kemper's pro team. Basich started snowboarding in 1985 and was only 17 when she competed in the 1987 World Snowboarding Championships. She came in sixth place. Basich quickly became known as one of the best female snowboarders in the world. Basich and fellow

The Backside 720

Tina Basich landed a new move in the half-pipe at the 1998 Winter X Games—the backside 720. The rider reaches the edge of the half-pipe and does two full backward turns, landing close to the edge again. Basich was the first woman to complete this trick successfully in competition. She won the gold and made snowboarding history.

▲ *The silver, gold, and bronze medalists from the first women's Olympic half-pipe competition in 1998 (left to right): Norwegian Stine Brun Kjeldaas, German Nicola Thost, and American Shannon Dunn.*

snowboarder Shannon Dunn came out with their own snowboard designs in 1994. These boards were the first of their kind, made just for female snowboarders.

At the time, competitions had more events for men than women. It was thought that women could not do the big jumps that men were doing. Basich and Dunn challenged that opinion at the 1994 Air & Style Big Air competition. In front of 15,000 people, these women cleared the 60 foot (18.3 m) jump. Because there was no official competition for women, their performances were not judged. However, the media later reported that they had done better than some of the men.

CHAPTER 6

GAME ON

The Olympic Winter Games were first televised in 1956, exposing people worldwide to skiing events. The first ski magazine debuted in 1936, and ski magazines were widely read from the 1950s and 1960s on. The first snowboarding magazine, *Absolutely Radical*, came out in March 1985. Some female athletes in skiing and snowboarding became favorites of the media and the fans, including Suzy Chaffee, Picabo Street, and Kelly Clark.

DANCING DOWN MOUNTAINS

The daughter of a ski jumper and an alpine skier, Suzy Chaffee was on the slopes by age two. As a child, she also studied classical ballet. Chaffee joined the U.S. Alpine Ski Team in 1965. Then, in 1967, she placed fourth in the World Ski Championships in Chile. After the 1968 Olympic Winter Games, Chaffee decided to switch to the new skiing style—freestyle.

Freestyle combined Chaffee's alpine skiing and dancing skills. She concentrated on ski ballet, now called acro. In the early 1970s, there was not a separate freestyle event for women. Chaffee competed against the men and won three World Championships titles in a row.

Suzy Chapstick

In 1978, Chapstick found a new spokesperson for its commercials—Suzy Chaffee. In the commercials, Chaffee skied into view and said, "Hi! I'm Suzy Chapstick!" These commercials made her a national celebrity. Soon, Chaffee was making more than $100,000 a year in endorsements from toothpaste and yogurt companies. She even designed her own skis with the Hart Ski Company in 1983.

Fans loved watching Chaffee as she danced down the mountains. She wore beautiful ski outfits and had amazing athletic skills. She was the face of freestyle skiing in the 1970s. Chaffee used her popularity to promote equal rights for women athletes and skiing for kids.

A SKIING PERSONALITY

The 1990s saw the rise of a female skiing superstar—Picabo Street. She began skiing at a young age but did not start alpine racing until high school. Street was daring and fast from the beginning—the perfect combination for alpine racing.

Street made the U.S. Ski Team in 1989 at the age of 17. She won the silver in the downhill event at the 1994 Olympics, and she won six of nine World Cup downhill races in 1995. Street won the World Cup title that year, becoming the first U.S. woman to do so. After a terrible

Hometown Hero

Cross-country skiing does not receive the same kind of attention as downhill and freestyle skiing. Cross-country races are long and go through isolated areas. However, cross-country skier Stefania Belmondo became a hero in her hometown of Pontebernado, Italy. When Belmondo competed in the 1992 Olympics, half of her hometown came to support her. In the final cross-country event, Belmondo won the gold.

knee injury in 1997, Street trained hard to get back on the slopes. She returned in 1998 to win an Olympic gold in super-G.

Street was famous. She appeared on television in *Sesame Street* and *American Gladiators*. She became the first skier to design a shoe with the Nike athletic company, called the Air Max Electrify. Street worked with United Airlines and Chapstick as well. Her bubbly personality and **determination** as an athlete made her a favorite with fans and the media.

SERIOUS SNOWBOARDER

A star from the 2002 Olympic Winter Games was Kelly Clark. She began snowboarding when she was only eight years old. As a kid, she did jumps and spins off ramps built in the woods. She also started a snowboarding club in fourth grade.

In 2002, when Clark was 18 years old, she went to the Olympics. In a practice run three days before the final, she took a bad fall, bruising her tailbone and breaking her wrist. Despite her injuries, Clark won the gold medal in the Olympic half-pipe event. This was the first U.S. gold medal in snowboarding for men or women. Clark continued to compete well, winning the 2004–05 World Cup title. She returned to the Olympics in 2006 and placed fourth. That same year, she won the gold at the Winter X Games. In 2010, she took gold in super-pipe

The Frontside 900

Kelly Clark was trailing Hannah Teter in the snowboarding competition in the 2006 Olympics. Clark had to decide: Should she do an easy trick she knew she could perform well and win the bronze or silver medal? Or should she try a risky trick and either win the gold or nothing at all, depending on how well she performed? Clark gave it all she had. The first five tricks of her run were impressive, but the next trick did not work out. She tried a frontside 900 (rotating forward two-and-one-half times) but was unable to land it. Clark came in fourth, but her run was thought to be one of the best by a woman.

(a taller and steeper half-pipe event) at the Winter X Games and bronze in half-pipe at the Olympics.

These are just a few of the women who helped bring skiing and snowboarding to the mainstream. They have led the way for the sports' huge growth in popularity.

▲ Kelly Clark completes a jump during the half-pipe competition at the 2002 Olympics, where she won the gold.

▲ Lindsey Vonn won a gold and a bronze medal at the 2010 Winter Olympics.

CHAPTER 7

PLAYING TO WIN

To become the best in any sport takes incredible skill, determination, and passion. Many female athletes have worked hard to become today's snowboarding and skiing champions.

LINDSEY VONN: ALPINE SKIING

A skier from the age of two, Lindsey Vonn became one of the world's top female alpine skiers. She started skiing at a small ski area in Burnsville, Minnesota. She showed so much talent that her family moved to Vail, Colorado, when she was ten. There, she had the opportunity to ski on more challenging slopes and improve her racing skills. After the move, Vonn soon took home national and international youth skiing awards.

Vonn has an impressive record. As of 2010, she had won three consecutive overall World Cup titles (2007–08, 2008–09, and 2009–10) and had 33 World Cup wins. In 2009, she also won two World Championship titles in her best events—downhill and super-G. In the 2010 Olympic Winter Games, she won a gold medal in downhill and a bronze medal in super-G.

Vonn's Hero

One of Vonn's heroes is Picabo Street. When Vonn was a teenager, she met Street at a book signing in Minneapolis, Minnesota. That meeting had a huge impact on the young Vonn. She decided that she wanted to compete in the Olympics, just like her hero. Vonn competed in her first Olympics in 2002. Since then, she and Street have been close friends.

Maria Riesch races to a second-place finish in the super-combined event at the 2010 Olympics.

MARIA RIESCH

German skier Maria Riesch is not only Lindsey Vonn's biggest competition but also her best friend. Riesch started skiing at the age of three and was very accomplished by the time she was 16. She won seven medals in the Junior World Championships between 2001 and 2003. At age 18 in 2003, she placed fifth in the World Championships. She had two knee injuries between 2004 and 2005 that stalled her career. But in 2008, she overcame her injuries and began competing at the top level again.

Riesch met Vonn in 2000 at the Junior World Championships. They became good friends three years later. They shared similar passions and interests. The two have taken vacations together, and Vonn has often spent Christmas in Germany with Riesch and her family.

Both women are fierce competitors. Riesch came in second to Vonn for the 2009 World Cup overall title. At the 2010 Olympics, Riesch took home gold medals in the slalom and the super-combined. In March 2010, she won her second slalom World Cup title in a row.

▲ Skier Hannah Kearney won the gold medal in moguls at the 2010 Olympics.

HANNAH KEARNEY: SKIING MOGULS

Vermont native Hannah Kearney has enjoyed the thrill of skiing freestyle and moguls since she was very young. She took first place in the moguls at the World Championships in 2005 and was a favorite going into the 2006 Olympics. However, a stumble dropped her to a 22nd-place finish.

Injuries kept Kearney out of skiing for most of 2006 through 2008, but she came back forcefully in 2009 to win the overall World Cup in moguls that year. Coming strong into the 2010 Olympics, Kearney took the first U.S.

gold medal of the games. She won five World Cup events in the 2009–10 season. She did not earn enough points, however, to beat Canada's Jennifer Heil, her long-time rival in the moguls.

JUSTYNA KOWALCZYK: CROSS-COUNTRY

European women have long been champions in cross-country skiing. Justyna Kowalczyk, a cross-country skier from Poland, has done well in both sprint and distance races. She won the bronze medal in the 30K (18.6 mile) race at the 2006 Olympic Winter Games. This was the first medal in cross-country skiing for her country.

Since then, Kowalczyk has had even greater achievements. She was the overall champion at the 2008–09 and

Sarah Will: Paralympics

Sarah Will was training to compete in the Olympics in alpine skiing in 1988 when she was paralyzed from the waist down in a skiing accident. Refusing to be slowed down, Will soon learned to ski in a seated position using a mono-ski. A mono-ski consists of a seat attached to a single ski. Between 1992 and 2002, Will won one silver and 12 gold medals in the **Paralympics**. Will was inducted into the U.S. Olympic Hall of Fame in 2009 and the U.S. Skiing Hall of Fame in 2010.

the 2009–10 World Cups. She also won two gold medals at the 2009 World Championships. At the 2010 Olympics, Kowalczyk took home three medals—a bronze in the 15K (9.3 mile) pursuit, a silver in the individual sprint classic, and a gold in the 30K (18.6 mile).

LINDSEY JACOBELLIS: SNOWBOARDING

As an admiring little sister, Lindsey Jacobellis wanted to snowboard just like her big brother Ben. She grew up to be one of the best snowboard cross athletes in the world.

At the 2006 Olympic Winter Games, she won the silver in snowboard cross. This was her first Olympics and also the first time snowboard cross was an Olympic event. Jacobellis won gold in snowboard cross at the 2005 and 2007 World Championships and at the Winter X Games in 2003, 2004, 2005, 2008, 2009, and 2010. She also competed in the slopestyle and half-pipe events.

A snowboard cross favorite going into the 2010 Olympics, Jacobellis did not win a medal. She was disqualified because she went out of bounds. She proved herself again, however, in March 2010, when she beat the Olympic snowboard cross champion, Canada's Maelle Ricker. This win was Jacobellis's 21st World Cup win. As of 2010, she also had two overall World Cup victories and two world titles.

TORAH BRIGHT: SNOWBOARDING

Torah Bright, an Australian athlete, started skiing at age two. She switched to snowboarding at age 11.

Bright's best event was the half-pipe, where she could perform amazing tricks. She won the gold in half-pipe at the 2007 Winter X Games, and she finished first at the 2008 U.S. Open. At the 2010 Olympics, she earned the gold, beating U.S. rival Hannah Teter, the 2006 Olympic gold medalist.

Today, snowboarding and skiing are just as much women's sports as men's. The best female athletes push the limits of these sports. These women have determination and talent, making them tough athletes and competitors. Snowboarding and skiing can be dangerous, but women athletes face the challenge and play hard. They also make sure to have fun on the ride!

▲ *Australian snowboarder Torah Bright won the gold medal in half-pipe at the 2010 Olympics.*

GLOSSARY

alpine: Any kind of downhill skiing; relating to high mountains.

camber: The arched shape at the middle of a ski.

carve: Making a turn at an angle.

corset: An undergarment for women that fits tightly around the waist and chest, holding them in.

determination: Having a strong purpose for doing something.

downhill: Skiing down mountains; in skiing competitions, the downhill event is the fastest and has the fewest gates.

elite: Among the very best in a group or category.

fall line: The straightest way down a hill.

fiberglass: A material made of glass fibers mixed with plastic.

gates: Markers that indicate the ski or snowboard course.

giant slalom: An alpine skiing event that has the second highest number of gates.

half-pipe: A terrain-park feature with two steep ramps and a valley in the middle.

hips: A terrain-park feature shaped like the letter A with steep, rounded walls and a flat top in the middle.

insulated: Covered or protected from extreme temperatures.

marathons: Long races.

media: Forms of communicating information, such as television, radio, print, and the Internet.

moguls: Bumps in a ski or snowboard course; in competition, mogul events are races that include jumps and tricks.

Nordic: Cross-country skiing.

Paralympics: International sporting event held immediately following each Olympic Games in which elite athletes with disabilities compete.

perseverance: Trying to do something despite problems.

quarter-pipe: A steep ramp; one half of a half-pipe.

rails: Terrain park features used for sliding.

rotation: A spin; a single full rotation is 360 degrees.

slalom: To ski or zigzag between gates; in competition, the slalom event has the most gates.

slopestyle: A snowboarding race including jumps, rails, hips, and a half-pipe or quarter-pipe.

snowboard cross: A race with jumps and turns.

super-combined: An alpine skiing event that includes one downhill and one slalom race.

super-G: An alpine skiing event that has the second fewest gates.

terrain parks: Areas for snowboarders to practice tricks, often including ramps, jumps, rails, and other features.

wicking fabric: Special fabric that pulls water away from a person's skin.

FOR MORE INFORMATION

BOOKS

Burns, Kylie. *Alpine and Freestyle Skiing*. New York: Crabtree, 2010.
This book features the history and fun facts about alpine and freestyle skiing at the Olympic Winter Games.

Burns, Kylie. *Biathlon, Cross-Country, Ski Jumping, and Nordic Combined*. New York: Crabtree, 2010.
This book explains the history of biathlon, cross-country skiing, ski jumping, and Nordic combined at the Olympic Winter Games.

Gustaitis, Joseph. *Snowboard*. New York: Crabtree, 2010.
This book includes trivia and history about snowboarding at the Olympic Winter Games.

Lawson, Peter. *Let's Go Skiing!* Bath, UK: Brown Dog Books, 2009.
This book features technical details, step-by-step photos, and diagrams to help skiers learn new skills.

Macy, Sue. *Freeze Frame: A Photographic History of the Winter Olympics*. Washington DC: National Geographic Children's Books, 2006.
This book uses photos to explore the history of the Olympic Winter Games through 2002.

Murdico, Suzanne. *Snowboarding: Techniques and Tricks*. New York: Rosen, 2003.
This book includes a history and overview of snowboarding and features discussions of the sport's equipment, tricks, and competitions.

WEB SITES

KidsHealth
Winter Sports: Sledding, Skiing, Snowboarding, Skating
kidshealth.org/kid/watch/out/winter_sports.html
This Web site features information about staying safe while
having fun with winter sports.

Lids on Kids
www.lidsonkids.org/home.asp
This Web site includes specific rules and resources about skiing
and snowboarding safety and responsibilities.

PBS Kids
Kids World Sports: Games: Snowboard Savage
pbskids.org/kws/games/snowboardsavage/
Do the best tricks in this snowboarding game to get the highest
score.

SnowMonsters
www.snowmonsters.com
This Web site includes games and information for skiers and
snowboarders.

INDEX

PLACES TO VISIT

1932 & 1980 Winter Olympic Museum

2634 Main Street, Lake Placid, NY 12946-3648
518-523-1655
www.whiteface.com/activities/museum.php
Located in the Olympic Center at Lake Placid, the 1932 & 1980
Winter Olympic Museum features exhibits and memorabilia
from the two Winter Olympics held there.

U.S. National Ski and Snowboard Hall of Fame and Museum

610 Palms Avenue, Ishpeming, MI 49849
906-485-6323
www.skihall.com
The U.S. National Ski and Snowboard Hall of Fame and Museum
honors U.S. skiers and snowboarders for athletic excellence. It
features a museum of skiing and snowboarding history.

ABOUT THE AUTHOR

Karen Latchana Kenney is the author of more
than 60 educational books for children and young
adults. When not reading or writing, she enjoys
biking around the lakes of Minneapolis with her
husband and son.

ABOUT THE CONTENT CONSULTANT

Frida Waara believes you must ski to see the
most precious places on this planet. So far that
includes the Geographic North Pole and slopes
on five of the seven continents. She'll soon add
Antarctica and the South Pole to her list. She
writes about snowsports and serves on the
board of the U.S. National Ski & Snowboard Hall
of Fame. She met her husband on skis, and their children make
a living skiing and snowboarding the peaks of the world.